TABLE OF CONTENTS

TABLE OF CONTENTS 2

1. ROAST LEG OF LAMB 4

2. SPRING LAMB RAGÙ 5

3. SPINACH-AND-ARTICHOKE CROWN ROAST OF LAMB...6

4. SLOW-COOKER EASTER LAMB 7

5. LAMB MEATBALLS 8

6. GRILLED LAMB SKEWERS WITH COUSCOUS TABBOULEH 9

7. LAMB BURGERS WITH MINT GREEN TEA PESTO 10

8. CUMIN LAMB NOODLES WITH EGGPLANT 12

9. SPICED LAMB (OR BEEF!) DUMPLINGS 13

10. GRILLED ROSEMARY LAMB MEATBALLS 14

11. GREEK LAMB, ORZO, AND SPINACH SALAD 15

12. PASTA WITH LAMB AND PECORINO 16

13. BUTTERMILK WAFFLES...17

14. BUCKWHEAT GALETTES WITH HAM & EGG 18

15. BABKA MONKEY BREAD 19

16. SPINACH & CHEESE QUICHE 20

17. TIRAMISU-STUFFED FRENCH TOAST 21

18. CROQUE MONSIEUR BREAKFAST CASSEROLE 22

19. BRIOCHE FRENCH TOAST 23

20. ITALIAN SAUSAGE & PEPPER FRITTATA AFFOGATO 24

21. BEST-EVER HOT CROSS BUNS 25

22. BLUEBERRY-LEMON RICOTTA STUFFED FRENCH TOAST..27

23. POTATO CHIP FRITTATA 28

24. CAPIROTADA 29

25. CRESCENT BREAKFAST TART 30

26. BLUEBERRY MONKEY BREAD 31

27. BRUSSELS SPROUTS HASH..33

28. BAGELS AND LOX 34

29. OVERNIGHT FRENCH TOAST 35

30. EGG & HASH BROWN CASSEROLE 36

31. AIR FRYER SPINACH, ROASTED RED PEPPER, AND GOAT CHEESE OMELET 37
32. BUTTERMILK PANCAKES 38
33. CLASSIC COFFEE CAKE 39
34. BEST-EVER CREAMY SCRAMBLED EGGS 40
35. CRESCENT BREAKFAST SQUARES 41
36. EASTER BREAD 42
37. INSTANT POT HASH 43
38. MONTE CRISTO SANDWICH 45
39. BREAKFAST STRATA 45
40. SOUR CREAM COFFEE CAKE 46
41. CLASSIC CINNAMON ROLLS 48
42. LEMON BLUEBERRY BABKA 49

1. ROAST LEG OF LAMB

PREP TIME:15 mins

TOTAL TIME:2 hrs 30 mins

Ingredients

- 1/4 c. + 1 tbsp extra-virgin olive oil, + more greasing
- 3 cloves garlic, chop up
- 1 tbsp. chop up rosemary, + 2 sprigs
- 1 tbsp. chop up thyme
- 1 (6 lb.) leg of lamb
- kosher salt
- Freshly ground black pepper
- 2 heads garlic, cloves peel off
- 8 oz. cipollini onions
- 2 lemons, halved

Directions

1. Oven temperature is 400 degrees. Mix 1/4 cup of oil, chop up garlic, rosemary, and thyme in a small bowl.
2. Put the lamb in a big roasting pan and season it with salt and pepper all over.
3. Step 3Apply herb oil to the lamb all over (you won't use it all at once). 30-minute roast.
4. Meanwhile, mix 1 tbsp oil, salt, and pepper in a larger bowl with the whole garlic cloves, onions, rosemary sprigs, and lemons.
5. Bake at 350 degrees. Wrap the lamb in extra herb oil after evenly distributing the garlic, onions, rosemary, and lemon halves. When the thickest section of the roast registers between 145° and 150° on a meat thermometer, add 1/4 cup of water to the roasting dish and cook for an additional 1 to 1 12 hours.
6. Before to sliceting and serving, let the lamb 15 minutes to rest.

2. SPRING LAMB RAGÙ

PREP TIME:10 mins

TOTAL TIME:35 mins

Ingredients

- 2 tbsp. extra-virgin olive oil
- 1 large leek, cleaned and thinly split (about 1½ c.) or 1 yellow onion, lightly chop up
- Kosher salt
- 3 cloves garlic, chop up
- 3 oil-packed anchovies
- 2 tsp. fresh rosemary, lightly chop up
- 1 tbsp. tomato paste
- 1 lb. ground lamb
- Freshly gound black pepper
- 1/2 c. white wine
- 1 1/2 c. chicken stock (you may need up to 2 c.)
- 12 oz. pappardelle or tagliatelle
- 2 tbsp. butter
- 3 oz. pea shoots, arugula or other baby green
- 2 tsp. lemon zest
- Juice of 1 lemon
- 1/2 c. loosely packed fresh herbs, such as parsley, mint, and split chives
- Pecorino, grated for serving

Directions

1. Heat the oil over medium heat in a 12-inch Dutch oven or skillet with deep sides. Cook the leek for 4 to 5 minutes, or until it is tender and transparent. Use salt to season.

2. Garlic, anchovies, rosemary, and tomato paste should all be stirred in at this point. Cook for 1 to 2 minutes, or until the anchovies have melted and the tomato paste has somewhat roasted.

3. Step 3: Add the lamb and cook for 5 to 7 minutes, pushing the meat firmly into the bottom of the pan until it starts to crisp. Add salt and pepper as need.

4. Pour in the wine and heat until it has reduced by half, about 3 minutes. While preparing the pasta, add 112 cups of the chicken stock to the sauce and let it simmer, stirring occasionally. Stir in the final 1/2 cup of stock if it appears to be drying out.

5. Large saucepan of salted water should be brought to a boil. Pasta should be cooked as directed on the package, but not quite al dente. When draining, save 1 cup of the cooking water.

6. Add the pasta, butter, and pea shoots to the skillet with the lamb. Stir until the pasta is shiny with sauce, the pea shoots are wilted, and the butter is melted, adding a few tbsp of the pasta cooking water you saved if it's necessary.

7. Add the remaining zest, all of the herbs, and a generous squeeze of lemon juice, then toss once more. Add the remaining herbs to the serving bowls on the plate. Add some cheese shavings to the dish.

3. SPINACH-AND-ARTICHOKE CROWN ROAST OF LAMB

PREP TIME:20 mins

TOTAL TIME:1 hr 35 mins

Ingredients

- 1 tbsp. chop up fresh oregano
- 1 tbsp. chop up fresh rosemary
- kosher salt
- Freshly ground black pepper
- 1 crown of Frenched lamb (prepared by your butcher)
- 2 tbsp. extra-virgin olive oil, + more for drizzling
- 2 c. basmati or jasmine rice
- 1 15-oz. can artichoke hearts
- 3 c. baby spinach, chop up

- 1/2 c. crumbled feta
- Juice of 1 large lemon
- 2 lemons, split, for serving

Directions

1. Set the oven to 375 degrees. Mix the oregano, rosemary, and salt & pepper in a small bowl. Apply a combination of olive oil and herbs all over the lamb crown.

2. Put the lamb in a Bundt pan so that the pan's center extends through the center of the crown. Place on a baking sheet and roast for 38 to 40 minutes, or until the internal temperature of the meat reaches 130°. Remove from Bundt pan, wrap in foil, and allow to sit for 15 minutes.

3. Cook the rice as directed on the packet in the interim. Place in a bowl with the artichokes, spinach, feta, lemon juice, salt, and pepper. Olive oil should be liberally drizzled before returning to the rice cooker to provide warmth while the lamb is resting.

4. Rice should be placed both inside the lamb crown and on the serving tray when it is time to serve. Serve after arranging lemon slices on a plate.

4. SLOW-COOKER EASTER LAMB

TOTAL TIME: 5 hrs

Ingredients

- 4 lb. lamb shanks
- kosher salt
- McCormick Pure Ground Black Pepper
- 2 tsp. McCormick Ground Mustard
- 1 tbsp. vegetable oil
- 1 large yellow onion, split into rounds
- 3 medium carrots, peel off and slice into thirds
- 2 garlic cloves, thinly split
- 3 fresh sprigs rosemary
- 4 c. beef broth, separated
- Freshly chop up parsley, for garnish

FOR GRAVY:

- 1 tbsp. butter
- 1 shallot, chop up
- 1 packet McCormick Original Country Gravy Mix
- 1 c. whole milk

Directions

1. Kosher salt, McCormick Pure Ground Black Pepper, and McCormick Ground Mustard are used to season the lamb shanks all over. Add oil to a big skillet set over medium heat, then sear the lamb all over.

2. Add onion, carrots, and grilled lamb to your slow cooker. Pour 3 cups of broth over the garlic and rosemary.

3. Cook, covered, for 9 hours on low or 4 12 to 5 hours on high, until tender. Take out of the crockpot and sit for 10 minutes.

4. Melt butter in a small pot over medium heat to prepare gravy. Add the shallot and sauté for 1 to 2 minutes, or until aromatic. Turn the heat down to low, add the McCormick Original Country Gravy Mix, and swirl to mix. While whisking frequently, add milk and the remaining broth to the pan. After simmering the mixture for one minute, turn off the heat.

5. Dress lamb with parsley and serve with gravy.

5. LAMB MEATBALLS

PREP TIME:20 mins

TOTAL TIME:50 mins

Ingredients

FOR THE MEATBALLS

- 1 lb. ground lamb
- 1 large egg, lightly beaten
- 3 cloves garlic, chop up
- 2 tbsp. freshly chop up parsley
- 2 tsp. freshly chop up oregano
- 1 tsp. ground cumin
- 1 tsp. kosher salt

- 1/2 tsp. freshly ground black pepper
- 1/4 tsp. crushed red pepper flakes
- 3 tbsp. extra-virgin olive oil

FOR THE GREEN GODDESS SAUCE

- 1 1/2 c. Greek yogurt
- 1/2 c. mayonnaise
- 1 1/2 c. basil leaves
- 1/2 c. parsley leaves
- 1/4 c. freshly chop up chives
- 1/4 c. fresh oregano leaves
- Juice of 1 lemon
- 2 cloves garlic
- Kosher salt

Freshly ground black pepper

Directions

1. the oven to 425 degrees. Using parchment paper, line a sizable baking sheet. Ground lamb, egg, garlic, parsley, oregano, cumin, salt, pepper, and red pepper flakes should all be mixd in a big bowl. Place on baking pans that have been prepped. Shape into 16 meatballs.
2. Oil the meatballs and bake for 20 minutes, or until brown and thoroughly done.
3. Make sauce in the meantime: Blend yogurt, mayonnaise, basil, parsley, chives, oregano, lemon juice, and garlic in a food processor. Add any other herbs as need and adjust with salt and pepper.
4. Warm meatballs should be served with green goddess sauce on the side.

6. GRILLED LAMB SKEWERS WITH COUSCOUS TABBOULEH

PREP TIME:25 mins

TOTAL TIME:40 mins

Ingredients

- 1 10 oz. box couscous
- 1 1/2 c. plain low-fat yogurt
- 1 tbsp. + 1 tsp. cumin
- 2 garlic cloves, chop up
- Juice of 2 lemons
- kosher salt
- Freshly ground black pepper
- 1 1/2 lb. leg of lamb, slice into 1 1/2 in. chunks
- 2 tomatoes, seeded and diced
- 1/2 English cucumber, halved, seeded, and diced
- 1/2 small red onion, lightly chop up
- 1/4 c. Lightly chop up fresh parsley
- 1/4 c. lightly chop up fresh mint
- 3 tbsp. extra-virgin olive oil
- Lemon wedges, for serving

Directions

1. Cook the couscous as directed on the bag, then fluff with a fork.

2. Mix yogurt, cumin, garlic, and half the lemon juice in a large bowl. Add salt and pepper as need. Stir in lamb after adding it.

3. Mix tomatoes, cucumber, red onion, parsley, mint, and couscous in a separate, large bowl. Salt the mixture after adding the remaining olive oil and lemon juice. Stir to mix.

4. Lamb is skewered on 6-inch sticks and then placed on a big dish. (There should be around 8 skewers total, each with 4 pieces of meat.) Add salt and pepper as need and then throw away any leftover marinade.

5. Grill or grill pan should be lightly oiled before being heated to smoking. For medium- to medium-rare, add the skewers and cook, flipping once, for 8 minutes.

6. Serve lamb skewers with lemon-flavored couscous tabbouleh.

7. LAMB BURGERS WITH MINT GREEN TEA PESTO

Ingredients

BURGERS

- 2 tbsp. shallot, chop up
- 2 tbsp. fresh flat-leaf parsley, chop up
- 1 tbsp. fresh mint, chop up
- 1 clove garlic, chop up
- 2 lb. ground lamb
- kosher salt and freshly ground pepper
- 6 pita rounds
- arugula

PESTO

- 1 c. loosely packed fresh mint leaves
- 1 c. fresh cilantro
- 4 tbsp. slivered toasted almonds
- 3/4 c. extra-virgin olive oil, + more if needed
- 1 bag Lipton Green Tea with Mint
- 1/2 c. crumbled feta cheese
- kosher salt and freshly ground black pepper

Directions

1. All items should be gently mixed in a bowl.
2. To fit pita, shape into 6 patties that are each about 12 inch thick.
3. Over a medium-high heat, warm the pan. Cook each patty while adding olive oil (about 5 minutes for medium).
4. Slice open the Lipton Green Tea with Mint tea bags and add the tea leaves to a food processor to make the pesto. Add toasted almonds, mint, and cilantro. Mix while gradually adding oil until a thin paste develops. Add the feta and pulse it once or twice to break it up. Add salt and pepper as need.

8. CUMIN LAMB NOODLES WITH EGGPLANT

TOTAL TIME: 30 mins

Ingredients

- 3 tbsp. extra-virgin olive oil
- 1 onion
- 1 medium eggplant
- 2 clove garlic
- 1 tsp. dried oregano
- 1 tsp. ground cumin
- 1/2 tsp. smoked paprika
- 1 pinch crushed red pepper
- kosher salt
- 3/4 lb. ground lamb
- 1/4 c. tomato paste
- 3/4 c. chicken stock
- 8 oz. gemelli
- 1/2 c. whole plain Greek yogurt
- c. Chop up mint

Directions

1. Oil should be heated in a big skillet. Add the onion and simmer for 5 minutes, stirring regularly, at a moderate heat. Salt and pepper should be added before adding the eggplant, garlic, oregano, cumin, paprika, and crushed red pepper. Cook while stirring for 1 minute or until aromatic. Lamb should be added and cooked while being chop up up with a wooden spoon. Cook the tomato paste for 2 minutes while stirring. Add the stock and stir, then bring to a boil. For 12 minutes, with the lid on, simmer the sauce over low heat until it thickens.

2. The following is a list of the most common questions we get from our customers. Save 1/2 cup of the pasta boiling water before draining. Add more water if you want a thinner sauce after you've added the pasta and 1/4 cup of the cooking water you've saved. Stir in the yogurt and mint after turning off the heat in the skillet. Serve hot and sprinkle with salt.

129. Roast Lamb

Total Time: 45 mins

Ingredients

SAVE RECIPE

- 1 lamb top round (1 1/4- to 1 1/2- lbs), trimmed
- Kosher salt and pepper
- 12 cloves garlic (4 cloves chop up)
- 1 tbsp. chop up rosemary
- 2 tsp. thyme leaves
- 2 pints grape tomatoes
- 2 tbsp. olive oil, separated
- Chop up parsley, for sprinkling

Directions

1. Heat oven to 400°F. Place lamb in roasting pan and season with 1 tsp salt and 1/2 tsp pepper.
2. Mix chop up garlic, rosemary, thyme, and 1 tbsp oil in a small bowl. Rub the meat, then cook for ten minutes.
3. Mix remaining tbsp of oil, 14 tsp of salt, and the tomatoes and garlic cloves. Around the meat, scatter the tomatoes and garlic, and roast for an additional 15 to 20 minutes, or until the internal temperature of the lamb reaches 125°F for medium-rare. Before slicing, move the lamb on a sliceting board and give it time to rest for at least 10 minutes. Garnish with parsley if wanted and serve with tomatoes and garlic.

9. SPICED LAMB (OR BEEF!) DUMPLINGS

Ingredients

SPICY LAMB DUMPLINGS

- 1 lb. ground lamb or ground beef

- 1/4 c. flat-leaf parsley, lightly chop up
- 1/4 c. mint, thinly split
- 1 tsp. ground cumin
- 1 tsp. sweet paprika
- Kosher salt
- Square dumpling wrappers (about 30)

GARLIC YOGURT SAUCE

- 1 c. whole-milk Greek yogurt
- 2 garlic cloves (grated)
- 1/4 tsp. salt

Directions

1. Produce filling: Lamb, parsley, mint, cumin, sweet paprika, and salt should be mixd.
2. One wrapper should have 1 rounded tbsp of filling in the center. Lightly moisten the wrapper's edges with water using your fingers. To thoroughly seal the dumpling, fold in the four corners to form a point, then tightly press the edges together. Move the sealed dumpling to a baking sheet covered with paper or flour. Repeat with the remaining wrappers and filling.
3. To a large pot of simmering water, add 1 tbsp of salt. Cook dumplings in three batches, tossing occasionally, for 3 to 6 minutes, or until the filling is well heated. Transfer to a plate lined with paper towels using a slotted spoon.
4. Creating Garlic Yogurt Sauce Salt, garlic, and yogurt are whisked together. Add lamb dumplings to the dish.

10. GRILLED ROSEMARY LAMB MEATBALLS

Prep Time: 10 mins

Total Time: 20 mins

Ingredients

- 1 lb. ground lamb
- 1/4 c. seasoned bread crumbs
- 2 cloves garlic, lightly chop up

- 2 tsp. lightly chop up fresh rosemary
- Kosher salt
- Freshly ground black pepper
- 4 medium tomatoes, chop up
- 8 oz. penne, cooked
- Chop up parsley, for garnish

Directions

1. Garlic, rosemary, bread crumbs, ground lamb, and 1/2 tsp each of salt and pepper are all mixd. Mixture should be separated into 16 lumps; gently roll into balls.
2. Cook covered over medium heat for 10 minutes, rotating once. Add tomatoes, penne, and 1/4 tsp salt to a bowl. Using parsley as a garnish, serve the meatballs over the penne.

11. GREEK LAMB, ORZO, AND SPINACH SALAD

PREP TIME:20 mins

COOK TIME:19 mins

TOTAL TIME:39 mins

INGREDIENTS

- 2 lemons
- 12 thin-slice rib lamb chops
- c. extra-virgin olive oil
- 1/4 c. fresh oregano leaves
- 2 clove garlic
- 1/2 tsp. salt
- 1/2 tsp. Pepper
- 1 c. dried orzo pasta
- 3/4 lb. eggplant
- 1 medium zucchini

- 1 medium yellow summer squash
- 1 red bell pepper
- 4 c. baby spinach
- 1 c. crumbled feta
- 1 medium red tomato
- 1 medium yellow tomato

DIRECTIONS

1. Slice one lemon into six pieces; keep the remaining lemon's juice and zest. Chops should be mixed with 1 tbsp of oil, 2 tsp of oregano, 2 tbsp of chop up garlic, and 1/4 tsp of salt and pepper. Preparing the grill and orzo while the marinade is at room temperature.

2. In the meantime, make pasta as directed on the package in a big pot of boiling water. Drain well, then rinse with cold water.

3. 2 tbsp of the oil should be brushed over the bell pepper, eggplant, zucchini, and squash. Turning often, grill vegetables for 14 minutes or until tender. To a chopping board, transfer. For medium-rare chops, grill them for 2 minutes on each side. Grill lemon slices for 1 minute. Stripe the grilled vegetables.

4. Put orzo in a large serving bowl; toss in saved lemon zest and juice, grilled veggies, spinach, feta, tomatoes, and the remaining oil, salt, and pepper. Add cooked chops on top.

12. PASTA WITH LAMB AND PECORINO

PREP TIME: 15 mins

TOTAL TIME: 30 mins

INGREDIENTS

- 1 lb. ground lamb
- 1 small red pepper
- 3 clove garlic
- 1 1/2 tsp. ground cumin
- 1 1/2 tsp. ground coriander
- 1 lb. penne rigate

- 3 tbsp. tomato paste
- 1 c. fresh mint leaves
- 1/2 c. grated Pecorino cheese

DIRECTIONS

1. Large covered saucepot of salted water should be heated to a rolling boil.
2. 12-inch skillet: medium-high heat. Salt the lamb with 1/2 a tsp after adding it. Sauté for 3 minutes, breaking up with back of wooden spoon until browned. Add red pepper, garlic, cumin, coriander, and a dash of salt. Cook for 3 minutes, turning regularly, or until the red pepper starts to soften.
3. Cook pasta as directed on the label in the meanwhile. 1 cup of the cooking water should be set aside. Pasta that has been drained should be added back to the pot. Add the saved pasta boiling water and tomato paste. 2 minutes of stirring cooking.
4. Toss the spaghetti in the pot with the pecorino, mint, and lamb mixture.

13. BUTTERMILK WAFFLES

PREP TIME:10 mins

TOTAL TIME:45 mins

Ingredients

- 2 c. all-purpose flour
- 1 tbsp. granulated sugar
- 2 tsp. baking powder
- 1 tsp. baking soda
- 1/2 tsp. kosher salt
- 2 eggs
- 2 c. buttermilk, shaken
- 1/2 c. (1 stick) butter, melted, + softened butter for serving
- Cooking spray
- Maple syrup and split fresh fruit, for serving

Directions

1. Mix the flour, sugar, salt, baking soda, and baking powder in a big bowl.

2. Whisk eggs, buttermilk, and melted butter in a medium bowl. Do not overmix; it's good if there are some lumps. Gently fold wet ingredients into dry ingredients until just mixd.

3. Apply cooking spray to a waffle iron that has been warmed. To completely cover the middle of the iron, pour about 1/2 cup of batter into it. Cook under cover for about 5 minutes, or until golden. Placing the waffle on a platter. Use the leftover batter to repeat.

4. Serve warm waffles topped with fruit, syrup, and softened butter.

14. BUCKWHEAT GALETTES WITH HAM & EGG

PREP TIME: 15 mins

TOTAL TIME: 55 mins

Ingredients

- 3/4 c. whole milk
- 1/4 c. all-purpose flour
- 1/4 c. buckwheat flour
- 8 large eggs, separated
- 4 tbsp. unsalted butter, 2 tbsp. melted, 2 tbsp. room temperature, separated
- Kosher salt
- 8 oz. very thinly split Black Forest-style ham
- 2 c. shredded Gruyère (about 8 oz.)
- Freshly ground black pepper

Directions

1. Set the oven to 375°. Mix milk, all-purpose flour, buckwheat flour, two eggs, two tbsp melted butter, and one-fourth tsp salt in a medium bowl.

2. Melt 1 tsp of butter in a 10" nonstick skillet over medium heat. Add a level 1/4 cup of batter, tilt the skillet, and swirl to spread the batter throughout the bottom of the pan in a uniform, thin layer. Sauté for about a minute, or until the galette is set and lightly browned in spots. Turn and continue to cook until firm and light golden on bottom side, 30 seconds to 1 minute more. Place on a platter. If galette is cooking too rapidly, lower heat to medium-low. Continue until you have 6 galettes using the remaining butter and batter, arranging them on a dish as you go.

3. Place each galette, one at a time, on a big baking sheet with a rim. Depending on how thinly the ham is slice, place around three slices on top, either aligning with the edge of the galette or barely dangling over the side. Galette's center should be covered with 1/3 cup of cheese. In the cheese, make a well. One egg should be cracked into a well and sprinkled with salt and pepper. Galette is folded up on four sides over the egg's white portion to form a square, leaving the yolk and some white visible. Then, arrange the remaining galettes, ham, cheese, and egg on the baking sheet side by side.

4. Bake for 13 to 15 minutes, or until the yolks are still runny and the eggs are barely set. Sprinkle with parsley and serve warm.

5. Galette batter can be prepared up to 12 hours in advance. Refrigerated bowl with a cover.

15. BABKA MONKEY BREAD

PREP TIME: 10 mins

TOTAL TIME: 1 hr 45 mins

Ingredients

- Unsalted butter, for pan
- 1/2 c. heavy cream
- 1/2 tsp. pure vanilla extract
- 1 c. (170 g.) semisweet chocolate chips
- 1/3 c. (30 g.) Dutch process dark cocoa powder
- 1/4 tsp. ground cinnamon
- 1/2 c. (100 g.) + 2 tbsp. granulated sugar, separated
- 2 (16.3-oz.) cans Original Pillsbury Grand Biscuits
- All-purpose flour, for dusting
- 1 tbsp. water

Directions

1. Set the oven to 375 degrees. Butter should be used to grease an ordinary loaf pan (8 1/2" by 4 1/2"). For further information, see the website.

2. Mix the chips, cocoa powder, cinnamon, and 1/2 cup of granulated sugar in a medium heatproof bowl. Blend the cream mixture until smooth before adding it to the chocolate mixture. Let to cool for ten minutes.

3. Each biscuit from 1 can should be rolled into a 9" long by 5" wide rectangle on a lightly dusted surface. Thinly layer the chocolate mixture over the top. Begin rolling into a log from the long end. Slice the log in half lengthwise, then in half crosswise. Twist each component by rotating it 90 degrees left and 90 degrees right (some chocolate mixture should be visible). Shape into a spherical by tucking in the edges, then place in the prepared pan (12 should snugly fit into bottom). Continue the process with the remaining dough and chocolate mixture, placing a second layer on top.

4. Bake bread for 55 to 1 hour, or until golden brown and no longer uncooked in the center, tenting with foil if it's browning too rapidly.

5. The remaining 2 tbsp of granulated sugar and water should be simmering in a separate small saucepan.

6. Apply sugar syrup to the babka. Let to to cool before serving.

16. SPINACH & CHEESE QUICHE

PREP TIME:15 mins

TOTAL TIME:1 hr 55 mins

Ingredients

- 1 homemade or store-bought 9" pie crust, defrosted according to package instructions
- 1 tbsp. extra-virgin olive oil
- 1 medium leek, cleaned well, halved lengthwise, and slice into ½" pieces (white and light green parts only)
- Kosher salt
- Freshly ground black pepper
- 5 oz. fresh spinach
- 1 1/2 c. shredded aged Gouda or white cheddar
- 1/4 c. thinly split scallions (from about 4 scallions)
- 1 medium shallot, chop up
- 2 large eggs
- 1 c. half-and-half

- Pinch freshly grated nutmeg (non-compulsory)

Directions

1. Set the oven to 375 degrees. Put the crust on the baking sheet, cover it with parchment paper, and stuff it with dried beans (or another pie weight). Bake for about 15 minutes, or until sides of crust are lightly brown and doughy appearance is gone. Reduce oven temperature to 325° and transfer to a wire rack to cool.

2. In the interim, warm the oil in a big skillet over medium heat. Salt and pepper the leeks after adding them. Cook 5 to 7 minutes, or until the greens are vibrant and tender. Add the spinach and simmer for approximately a minute, or until wilted. Add extra pepper and salt as need, then transfer to a bowl to chill.

3. Mix the cheese, scallions, and shallot in a medium bowl.

4. Eggs should be smoothed out in a sizable dish. Half-and-half should be incorporated before adding nutmeg, pepper, and, if using, salt.

5. When the spinach mixture and crust have reached room temperature, construct the quiche as follows: On the bottom of the pie crust, evenly distribute half of the cheese mixture. Add the spinach and leek mixture next, spreading it out evenly. Over spinach, pour egg mixture; top with remaining cheese mixture.

6. Quiche should bake for 40 to 45 minutes or until just set. Let to cool for about 20 minutes before serving warm.

17. TIRAMISU-STUFFED FRENCH TOAST

PREP TIME:15 mins

TOTAL TIME:40 mins

Ingredients

- 4 oz. mascarpone cheese
- 2 oz. cream cheese, softened
- 1/4 c. confectioners' sugar
- 1 loaf brioche, slice into 1 1/2"-thick slices (preferably day-old)
- 4 large eggs
- 1 1/2 c. whole milk
- 1/2 c. heavy cream

- 1/4 c. granulated sugar
- 2 tsp. instant espresso
- 1 tsp. pure vanilla extract
- 2 tbsp. (or more) unsalted butter
- Unsweetened cocoa powder and maple syrup, for serving

Directions

1. In a medium bowl, using a rubber spatula, whisk mascarpone, cream cheese, and confectioners' sugar until smooth. Transfer to a zip-top bag with the corner slice off or a piping bag with a medium round tip.

2. Slice a 2"-wide slit into the bottom of each slice of bread with a paring knife, entering the knife approximately as far as the blade, being careful not to slice through to the other side. Mascarpone filling is piped into incisions.

3. Whisk together the eggs, milk, cream, sugar, espresso, and vanilla in a big basin. Bread with filling should be dipped into the egg mixture and given a 10-second soak on each side.

4. Melt butter in a large skillet over medium heat until foaming. Cook bread in batches, turning it once, for about 3 minutes per side, or until golden brown. Continue the process with the remaining bread, adjusting the heat and including extra butter as necessary.

5. On a dish, arrange the French toast. Sprinkle with cocoa powder and serve alongside maple syrup.

18. CROQUE MONSIEUR BREAKFAST CASSEROLE

PREP TIME: 20 mins

TOTAL TIME: 1 hr 30 mins

Ingredients

- 1 large loaf country-style bread, slice into 1" cubes
- 6 large eggs
- 1 c. half-and-half
- 1/4 c. Dijon mustard
- Kosher salt
- Freshly ground black pepper

- 4 tbsp. unsalted butter, + more for pan
- 6 oz. shredded Gruyére (about 2 1/2 c.), separated
- 4 oz. ham, torn into 1" pieces, separated
- 1/4 c. (30 g.) all-purpose flour
- 2 1/2 c. whole milk
- Pinch of ground nutmeg

Directions

1. Preheat oven to 300°. Spread the bread in a uniform layer on a baking sheet, and bake for 10 to 15 minutes, or until it is crispy and dried out. Place in a large bowl.
2. Mix the eggs, half-and-half, and mustard in a big glass measuring cup of; season with salt and pepper. Pour over the toast and coat with a toss. Give 10 minutes to soak.
3. 350° is the recommended oven temperature. A 13" by 9" baking dish should be butter-greased. Half of the bread should be added to the dish. Top with 1 cup of Gruyére and half of ham. Add the last slice of bread on top and then the last of the liquid. Add the leftover ham and 1/2 cup of Gruyére on top.
4. Bake dish for 30 to 40 minutes, or until cheese is melted and bread is crispy and golden.
5. Meanwhile, melt butter in a medium pot over medium heat. Butter is whisked with flour added. Sauté for about 2 minutes, stirring regularly, or until browned and smelling nutty. While whisking, carefully pour in milk and continue to whisk until smooth. Bring to a simmer and cook, stirring regularly, for about a minute, or until sauce is just thick enough to coat a spoon but isn't gravy-thick. Salt and pepper as need; stir in nutmeg.
6. Heat the broiler. Place remaining 1 cup of Gruyére on top of the sauce-covered dish.
7. Watching carefully, broil for 2 to 5 minutes or until cheese is melted and beginning to turn brown.

19. BRIOCHE FRENCH TOAST

PREP TIME:10 mins

TOTAL TIME:45 mins

Ingredients

- 1 (1-lb.) loaf cinnamon twist or plain brioche, slice into 1"-thick slices
- 4 large eggs
- 1 c. whole milk
- 1/2 c. heavy cream

- 2 tbsp. granulated sugar
- 1 tsp. ground cinnamon
- 1 tsp. pure vanilla extract
- 1/4 tsp. ground nutmeg
- Kosher salt
- 3 tbsp. unsalted butter, separated, + more if needed
- Maple syrup, mixed berries, and confectioners' sugar, for serving (non-compulsory)

Directions

1. Set the oven to 200°. Arrange the bread in a single layer on a large baking sheet with a rim. It takes roughly 20 minutes to dry out bread in the oven. Cool down.

2. Mix the eggs, milk, cream, granulated sugar, cinnamon, vanilla, nutmeg, and a dash of salt in a sizable, shallow baking dish. Place the bread, two slices at a time, into the egg mixture and let it soak for 15 to 20 seconds on each side.

3. Melt 1 tbsp of butter over medium-low heat in a sizable skillet (ideally nonstick). Add the bread once it starts to sizzle. Sauté for 3 to 5 minutes on each side or until both sides are golden brown. Continue the process with the remaining bread, adjusting the heat and including extra butter as necessary.

4. Add a heavy drizzle of maple syrup before serving. If using, top with berries and dust with powdered sugar.

20. ITALIAN SAUSAGE & PEPPER FRITTATA AFFOGATO

PREP TIME: 20 mins

TOTAL TIME: 45 mins

Ingredients

- 12 large eggs
- 1/4 c. chop up fresh basil leaves, + more for serving
- 1/4 c. whole milk
- 1/2 tsp. kosher salt
- 1/4 tsp. freshly ground black pepper
- 2 tbsp. extra-virgin olive oil

- 1 medium red bell pepper, stemmed, seeded, and thinly split
- 1 small yellow onion, thinly split
- 1/2 lb. spicy or sweet Italian sausage, casings removed
- 2 c. store-bought or homemade marinara sauce
- 1 1/2 c. shredded mozzarella (about 6 oz.)

Directions

1. Turn the broiler on high. Mix the eggs, basil, milk, salt, and pepper in a medium bowl.

2. Heat oil in a 10" nonstick ovenproof skillet over medium-high heat. Add the bell pepper and onion, and simmer for 3 minutes, stirring periodically, until just tender. Place sausage on the other side of the skillet after pushing the vegetables to one side. Using a wooden spoon, crumble the sausage into tiny pieces. Stir in the veggies, then heat, stirring regularly, for 4 to 6 minutes, or until the sausage is golden brown and well cooked.

3. Put the egg mixture in the skillet with the vegetables and sausage. Sauté, slowly stirring with a spatula and scraping bottom and sides of skillet to make large curds, until eggs are almost set, 2 to 3 minutes. Form an even layer by spreading.

4. Move skillet to oven, then broil for three minutes, or until puffed and beginning to turn brown. Take out of the oven. Pour marinara over and sprinkle with mozzarella. Broil for an additional 3 to 5 minutes, or until cheese is melted and bubbling and sauce is heated. 5 minutes should pass before serving. Add some fresh basil.

21. BEST-EVER HOT CROSS BUNS

PREP TIME: 35 mins

TOTAL TIME: 3 hrs 35 mins

Ingredients

FOR THE ROLLS

- 1 c. whole milk, warm
- 2 (0.25-oz.) packages active dry yeast
- 1/2 c. granulated sugar
- 1/3 c. butter, melted
- 1 large egg yolk

- 1 tsp. pure vanilla extract
- 3 c. all-purpose flour, + more for kneading
- 1 tsp. kosher salt
- 1/2 tsp. ground cinnamon
- 1/4 tsp. ground nutmeg
- 1/2 c. dried currants, plumped in hot water then drained
- 1 tsp. lemon zest
- Egg wash, for brushing

FOR THE GLAZE

- 2 c. powdered sugar
- 2 tbsp. whole milk
- 1/2 tsp. lemon zest

Directions

1. Mix the milk, yeast, and a dash of sugar in a medium basin. Let it settle for 20 minutes or more without stirring until frothy. Add vanilla, egg yolk, and butter to the yeast mixture while whisking. Mix the flour, remaining sugar, salt, cinnamon, and nutmeg in a big bowl. The yeast mixture should be placed within the center-made well in the flour mixture. With a wooden spoon, mix the ingredients until a thick, shaggy dough forms. Add currants and stir.

2. The dough should be soft and elastic after 8 to 10 minutes of kneading it on a heavily floured surface. A big ball of dough should be formed.

3. Put the dough inside a big bowl that has been butter-greased. Cover with plastic wrap and allow to double in size for approximately 1 1/2 hours at room temperature.

4. Butter a 9" x 13" baking pan when the dough is ready to be shaped into rolls. The dough should be flipped over and patted into a sizable rectangle on a lightly dusted surface. Make 12 equal chunks of the dough using a pizza wheel or a sharp knife.

5. Place each piece seam-side-down into the butter pan after rolling each piece into a roll and tucking the edges under. Wrapped in plastic, leave the rolls to rise in a warm location for about 45 minutes, or until they have doubled in size.

6. Heat the oven to 375 degrees after the second rise. Bun tops should be egg-washed. Bake for 22 to 25 minutes, or until brown and fluffy.

7. Create glaze: Lemon zest, milk, and powdered sugar should be thoroughly mixd. Add to a medium resealable plastic bag and make a small incision in the corner of the bag. Over each bun, pipe a thick cross shape.

8. At room temperature or heated, serve.

Nutrition

(per serving): 321 calories, 6 g protein, 60 g Carbs, 2 g fiber, 33 g sugar, 7 g fat, 4 g Sat fat, 219 mg sodium

22. BLUEBERRY-LEMON RICOTTA STUFFED FRENCH TOAST

PREP TIME: 5 mins

TOTAL TIME: 40 mins

Ingredients

- 2 large eggs, whisked well
- 1/2 c. whole milk
- 1 tbsp. granulated sugar
- Kosher salt
- 1/4 tsp. Freshly grated nutmeg (non-compulsory)
- 2 slices sourdough bread, slice 1" thick
- 1/2 c. whole milk ricotta, + more for serving
- 1 tbsp. blueberry jam, + more for serving
- 1/4 c. fresh blueberries, + more for serving
- Zest of ½ medium lemon, + more for serving
- Powdered sugar, for serving (non-compulsory)

Directions

1. Use a fork to stir together the eggs, milk, sugar, a dash of salt, and nutmeg, if using, in an 8" or 9" square baking pan. By placing each slice of bread on its flat side and using a serrated knife to slice about 4 to 5 of the way down, you can create a pocket in each one. Continue with the second piece of bread.

2. Put bread in egg mixture and let soak for 10 minutes. After 10 more minutes of soaking, flip.

3. Make the ricotta filling in the interim: Ricotta, jam, fresh blueberries, lemon zest, and a dash of salt are mixed together in a medium basin. Distribute the mixture between the two bread pockets that have been soaked.

4. For further information, see the website. Toast should be added once the butter has stopped foaming. Sauté for 3 to 4 minutes, flip, and cook for another 3 to 4 minutes, or until golden brown.

5. Top with extra ricotta, jam, lemon zest, and fresh berries before serving.

23. POTATO CHIP FRITTATA

PREP TIME:5 mins

TOTAL TIME:55 mins

Ingredients

- 2 tbsp. extra-virgin olive oil
- 1/2 medium yellow onion, chop up
- 8 large eggs
- 1/4 c. sour cream, + more for garnish
- 1 1/2 c. sour cream & onion chips, + more for garnish
- 2 tbsp. freshly chop up chives, + more for garnish
- Kosher salt
- Freshly ground black pepper

Directions

1. Heat oil in a medium pan over medium heat while preheating the oven to 375 degrees. Add the onion and simmer for 20 to 25 minutes, stirring regularly, until they are brown and caramelized.

2. In the meantime, whisk together the sour cream and eggs in a large bowl. Stir in the chips and chives after adding them. Add salt and pepper after letting the dish settle for 10 minutes.

3. Pour egg mixture into skillet once onions are caramelized and whisk to spread potato chips evenly.

4. ssssssss a number of ins thess an in ss.

5. After five minutes of cooling, sprinkle with extra sour cream, chips, and chives before serving.

24. CAPIROTADA

PREP TIME: 5 mins

TOTAL TIME: 1 hr 10 mins

Ingredients

- 2 tbsp. unsalted butter, + more for pan
- 4 bolillo rolls or 1 large loaf plain French bread, slice into 1/2"- to 3/4"-thick slices
- 4 c. water
- 2 c. (430 g.) packed piloncilo or dark brown sugar
- 1 1/2 tsp. ground cinnamon
- 1/4 tsp. ground cloves
- 1/4 tsp. ground nutmeg
- Pinch of kosher salt
- 1/2 c. (45 g.) split almonds, separated
- 1/4 c. (45 g.) raisins, separated
- 1/4 c. (30 g.) dried apricots, thinly split, separated
- 3 oz. crumbled queso añejo or cotija cheese, separated

Directions

1. Butter-grease an 8" by 8" baking dish and preheat the oven to 400 degrees. Place a baking sheet inside a wire rack.
2. Place bread on a rack and bake for 15 to 17 minutes, or until the edges are crispy and gently golden brown. 350° is a good oven temperature to use.
3. In the meantime, heat water, piloncillo, cinnamon, cloves, nutmeg, salt, and the final 2 tbsp of butter in a medium pot over high heat. Simmer for about 10 minutes, stirring periodically, until somewhat reduced. Get rid of the heat.
4. Half of the bread should be layered in the dish's base. Sprinkle half of the cheese, raisins, apricots, and almonds on top of the syrup. On top, layer the remaining bread. Pour syrup over the bread until all of the dry patches are covered (there will be syrup left over). Add the remaining cheese, raisins, apricots, and almonds.

5. Bread pudding should be baked for around 30 minutes, adding more syrup if the pudding seems dry. Ten minutes should pass before serving.

25. CRESCENT BREAKFAST TART

PREP TIME:15 mins

TOTAL TIME:30 mins

Ingredients

- 1 can crescent dough
- 6 eggs
- 2/3 c. white cheddar
- 4 slices cooked bacon
- kosher salt
- Freshly ground black pepper
- 1 tbsp. Chop up chives, for garnish

Directions

1. Place parchment paper on a medium baking sheet and preheat the oven to 400 degrees. Put the crescent dough on the baking sheet and seal the seams.

2. To form a crust, fold the dough's edges in. Cheese and cracked eggs are sprinkled on crescent-shaped dough. Sprinkle salt and pepper all over the bacon before placing it on top.

3. Bake for 10 to 15 minutes, or until egg whites are set and crust is brown. Gently transfer baking sheet to oven.

4. Garnish with chives. Serve warm after sliceting into squares.

26. BLUEBERRY MONKEY BREAD

PREP TIME:20 mins

TOTAL TIME:3 hrs

Ingredients

DOUGH

- 3/4 c. (180 ml.) whole milk, heated to 110°
- 1/2 c. (120 ml.) water, heated to 110°
- 1/4 c. (49 g.) granulated sugar
- 2 tbsp. (28 g.) butter, melted, + more for bowl
- 2 1/4 tsp. (7 g.) active dry yeast
- 3 1/4 c. (390 g.) all-purpose flour
- 2 tsp. kosher salt

BLUEBERRY SAUCE

- 1 tbsp. granulated sugar
- 1 tbsp. water
- 2 c. (1 pt.) fresh or refrigeratedd blueberries, separated
- 1/2 tsp. cornstarch, dissolved in 1 tsp. cold water
- 1 tsp. fresh lemon juice
- Pinch of kosher salt

ASSEMBLY

- 1/2 c. (1 stick; 113 g.) unsalted butter, melted, + 2 tbsp. (28 g.) unsalted butter, softened, separated
- 1 c. (198 g.) brown sugar
- 2 tsp. ground cinnamon
- 1 tsp. ground cardamom
- 1/2 tsp. kosher salt
- All-purpose flour, for surface

- 1/4 c. (57 oz.) cream cheese
- 2/3 (80 g.) powdered sugar
- 1 tbsp. (or more) whole milk

Directions

DOUGH

1. Stir the milk, water, butter, and granulated sugar in a small heatproof bowl until the sugar is dissolved. Add the yeast, stir, and wait 5 to 10 minutes for it to froth.
2. Mix the flour and salt in a stand mixer's big bowl using the paddle attachment. Add the yeast mixture and blend on low speed. Change to the dough hook, increase the speed to high, and beat the dough for 6 to 8 minutes, or until it is smooth and elastic (it will be sticky).
3. Dough should be transferred to a butter-greased bowl. Cover and allow to grow until doubled, about one hour, in a warm environment.

THE BLUEBERRY SAUCE

1. One cup of blueberries, water, and granulated sugar should be heated in a small saucepan over medium heat while stirring occasionally, until the berries start to burst and the mixture comes to a boil. Lower heat to medium-low and simmer for 2 to 3 minutes, stirring regularly, until berries have reduced to a sauce. Cornstarch should be dissolved before adding it, and boil for a further minute or so to mix.
2. Add salt, lemon juice, and the remaining 1 cup of blueberries after removing from the heat. Cool down.
3. Plan ahead: Make the blueberry sauce three days in advance. Transfer to an airtight jar and chill after allowing to cool.

ASSEMBLY

1. A 12-cup of Bundt pan should be greased with 2 tsp of melted butter. In a small, flat container, add the remaining 6 tbsp of melted butter. Stir together brown sugar, salt, cinnamon, and cardamom in a different tiny flat container.
2. On a work area that has been lightly dusted with flour, roll out the dough. Create 36 equal pieces (about 20 g. each). Before rolling in spiced sugar, dip each piece in melted butter. In the bottom of the prepared pan, arrange 12 pieces. Add half the blueberry sauce on top. Continue layering, then add the final 12 pieces of dough on top.
3. Cover and allow to rise for 20 to 30 minutes, or until top dough balls almost touch the top of the mold.
4. Set the oven to 350 degrees while you wait. Bread should be baked for 35 to 45 minutes, or until it is thoroughly browned on top and around the edges (an instant-read thermometer placed into a ball

should read at least 190°). Let to cool for five minutes, then use a tiny knife to release the pan's edges. Onto a platter, invert.

5. Cream cheese and 2 tbsp softened butter should be thoroughly mixd in a medium basin. Add extra milk if necessary to achieve a smooth, pourable glaze as you stir in the powdered sugar and milk. . For that. For that. And for that. For that. And for that. For that. And for that.

6. Glaze can be prepared three days in advance. Refrigerated after transferring to an airtight container. When ready to use, microwave the glaze for 5 seconds at a time, stirring after each, until it reaches drizzling consistency.

27. BRUSSELS SPROUTS HASH

PREP TIME: 10 mins

TOTAL TIME: 40 mins

Ingredients

- 6 slices bacon, slice into 1" pieces
- 1/2 onion, chop up
- 1 lb. Brussels sprouts, trimmed and quartered
- Kosher salt
- Freshly ground black pepper
- 1/4 tsp. crushed red pepper flakes
- 2 cloves garlic, chop up
- 4 large eggs

Directions

1. Cook bacon until crispy in a large skillet over medium heat. Turn off the heat and transfer the bacon to a dish lined with paper towels. Remove all the bacon fat except for one tbsp.

2. Return the heat to medium, then stir in the onion and the Brussels sprouts. Vegetables should be cooked, occasionally tossing, until they start to soften and turn golden. Add salt, pepper, and red pepper flakes for seasoning.

3. Simmer skillet with 2 tbsp of water covered. Simmer until Brussels sprouts are tender and water has evaporated, about 5 minutes. (If the Brussels sprouts are not tender after adding extra water and covering the pan for a few more minutes.) Cook the garlic in the skillet for one minute, until fragrant.

4. Make four holes in the hash with a wooden spoon to show the skillet's bottom. Each hole should have an egg in it, which should be seasoned with salt and pepper. Return the lid and continue cooking the eggs for 5 minutes or until they are just set in the middle.

5. The entire skillet should be covered with fried bacon bits before serving.

28. BAGELS AND LOX

PREP TIME: 5 mins

TOTAL TIME: 10 mins

Ingredients

FOR SCALLION DILL CREAM CHEESE

- 2/3 cream cheese, slightly softened
- 3 scallions, thinly split
- 2 tsp. fresh dill, lightly chop up
- 2 tsp. lemon juice

FOR BAGEL AND LOX

- 2 bagels, split and toasted if desired
- 8 slices Lox, split paper thin
- 2/3 c. schmear, such as cream cheese, tofu spread or whitefish salad
- Thinly split tomato
- Thinly split cucumber
- Thinly split red onion
- Capers
- Fresh dill, for garnish

Directions

1. For the cream cheese, put the cream cheese, scallions, dill, and lemon juice in a medium bowl and stir until well incorporated.

2. To make the bagels: Each bagel slice should have an even layer of schmear. Add two lox slices, tomato, cucumber, red onion, and capers on the top. Open-faced bagels should be served with some fresh dill on top.

29. OVERNIGHT FRENCH TOAST

PREP TIME:15 mins

TOTAL TIME:13 hrs 5 mins

Ingredients

FRENCH TOAST

- 1 (1-lb.) loaf raisin challah or regular challah, split 1" thick
- 8 large eggs
- 1/2 c. light brown sugar
- 1 c. heavy cream
- 1 c. whole milk
- 1 tsp. vanilla extract
- 1/2 tsp. ground cinnamon
- 1/2 tsp. kosher salt
- 1/4 tsp. freshly grated nutmeg

TOPPING

- 1 c. (2 sticks) butter, softened
- 1 c. light brown sugar
- 1 c. raw pecans, roughly chop up
- 1/2 tsp. ground cinnamon
- 1/4 tsp. freshly grated nutmeg
- 1/4 tsp. kosher salt
- Fresh fruit and maple syrup, for serving

Directions

TOAST IN FRENCH

1. Slices should air dry for at least two hours, and ideally up to eight.

2. A 13" by 9" baking dish should be sprayed with cooking oil. Place slices in a baking dish in two rows that overlap.

3. Whisk eggs and brown sugar together in a big bowl until mixd. Cream, milk, vanilla, cinnamon, salt, and nutmeg are all whisked in. Pour egg mixture over bread in an equal layer using a ladle. Wrap foil tightly around the baking dish and place it in the refrigerator for up to 12 hours.

TOPPING

- the oven to 350 degrees. Mix the butter, brown sugar, pecans, cinnamon, nutmeg, and salt into a thick paste in a medium bowl.

- On the bread, spread the butter mixture evenly. Bake for 30 to 40 minutes, or until puffed and golden brown.

- Serve French toast with fruit and a generous amount of maple syrup.

30. EGG & HASH BROWN CASSEROLE

PREP TIME:15 mins

TOTAL TIME:1 hr 15 mins

Ingredients

- 1/4 c. extra-virgin olive oil, separated
- 1 lb. loose pork or turkey breakfast sausage
- 1 medium yellow onion, lightly chop up
- 1 medium red bell pepper, seeded, lightly chop up
- Kosher salt
- Freshly ground black pepper
- 2 cloves garlic, chop up
- 10 c. (packed) baby spinach (from 2 [5-oz.] containers)
- 1 (20-oz.) bag refrigeratedd shredded hash browns
- 8 large eggs
- 3/4 c. low-sodium chicken broth
- 1/2 c. sour cream
- 1 tbsp. Dijon mustard

- 1 tsp. hot sauce
- 8 oz. shredded cheddar (about 2 c.), separated

Directions

1. Set the oven to 375°. A 13" by 9" baking dish should be greased with cooking spray.

2. Heat one tbsp of oil in a sizable nonstick skillet over medium-high heat. Sausage takes around 3 minutes to brown and become well cooked when heated while being broken up with a wooden spoon. Transfer the sausage to a big bowl after draining any extra oil from the skillet.

3. 1 tbsp. oil is heated in the skillet at medium heat once more. For about 3 minutes, stir occasionally as you cook the onion, bell pepper, salt, and black pepper until the vegetables are softened and lightly browned. Add the garlic and stir-fry for approximately a minute, or until fragrant. When all the spinach is integrated and wilted, which takes another 3 minutes, add spinach in generous handfuls, tossing and cooking between each addition. Put the sausage in the bowl with the vegetable mixture.

4. Re-heat the skillet to medium-low and add the final 2 tbsp of oil. Hash browns should be cooked for 12 minutes, stirring occasionally, until crisp and golden. Scoop hash browns into bowl with sausage and vegetables.

5. Eggs, broth, sour cream, mustard, spicy sauce, 1/2 tsp. salt, and 1/2 tsp. black pepper should all be thoroughly blended in another big bowl. Add 1 cup of cheese and stir. Pour the hash brown mixture into the egg mixture after folding it in. Add the final 1 cup of cheese.

6. Bake for about 30 minutes, or until eggs are just set. Slice after cooling for five minutes and serve.

31. AIR FRYER SPINACH, ROASTED RED PEPPER, AND GOAT CHEESE OMELET

PREP TIME: 5 mins

TOTAL TIME: 15 mins

Ingredients

- Olive oil cooking spray
- 3 large eggs
- 2 tbsp. whole milk
- Kosher salt
- Freshly ground black pepper
- 3 tbsp. thawed and well-squeezed chop up refrigeratedd spinach

- 3 tbsp. lightly chop up roasted red peppers
- 1 tbsp. crumbled goat cheese

Directions

1. Use cooking spray to grease a 7" nonstick round cake pan. Eggs, milk, a generous tsp of salt, and a few grinds of black pepper should all be thoroughly blended in a medium bowl.

2. Add egg mixture to pan after preparation. Add spinach and red peppers to the top of the egg mixture in half. Transfer the pan carefully to the air fryer basket. Cook eggs for 6 to 8 minutes at 350° until they are barely set.

3. Air fryer pan should be removed. Goat cheese goes well with veggies. With a spatula, fold egg over filling. Out of the pan, slide the omelet onto a platter.

32. BUTTERMILK PANCAKES

PREP TIME:10 mins

TOTAL TIME:35 mins

Ingredients

- 2 c. all-purpose flour
- 2 1/2 tbsp. granulated sugar
- 1 tsp. baking powder
- 1 tsp. baking osda
- 1 tsp. kosher salt
- 2 1/2 c. buttermilk
- 2 eggs, separated
- 4 tbsp. unsalted butter, melted, + more for serving
- Vegetable oil, for cooking
- Maple syrup, for serving

Directions

1. Mix the flour, sugar, baking soda, baking powder, and salt in a medium bowl. Buttermilk and egg yolks should be whisked together in a different medium dish. Stream in the melted butter as you whisk.

2. Egg whites should be beaten on high speed in a separate bowl for one to two minutes, or until stiff peaks form, using an electric mixer with the whisk attachment. Just mix the egg whites with the wet ingredients. Next, add the wet ingredients on top of the dry and gently fold to blend (do not overmix). Some bumps are fine.

3. A griddle or other heavy bottomed skillet should be heated for two to three minutes on medium heat before using. Add about a tsp of oil, then work it into the frying surface with a cloth or paper towel until no oil is left.

4. Ladle as many heaping 13 cups of batter as you can fit onto the griddle using a measuring cup of. Next, use the bottom of the measuring cup of to carefully spread the batter into circles that are all the same size. Cook pancakes for 2 to 3 minutes, or until bubbles appear on the top and the sides begin to pull away from the pan. Next flip the pancakes over and cook for an additional 2 to 3 minutes, or until the bottom is brown and the top is fluffy. Move to a rack. Continue cooking the remaining batter in batches, cleaning the pan between each and adding extra oil.

5. Warm pancakes with butter and syrup should be served.

33. CLASSIC COFFEE CAKE

PREP TIME:20 mins

TOTAL TIME:1 hr 20 mins

Ingredients

FOR CAKE

- 3/4 c. (1 1/2 sticks) unsalted butter, softened to room temperature
- 1 1/4 c. granulated sugar
- 1/4 c. brown sugar
- 3 large eggs
- 1 1/4 c. sour cream
- 1 tsp. vanilla extract
- 2 1/4 c. all-purpose flour
- 1/4 c. cornstarch
- 2 tsp. baking powder
- 1/2 tsp. baking soda

- 1 tsp. kosher salt

FOR STREUSEL

- 1/2 c. packed light brown sugar
- 1 c. all-purpose flour
- 1 1/2 tsp. ground cinnamon
- Pinch nutmeg (non-compulsory)
- Pinch kosher salt
- 6 tbsp. butter, melted
- 3/4 c. toasted pecans, chop up

Directions

1. Place parchment paper in a 9" x 13" pan and preheat the oven to 350 degrees. Cream the butter and sugars in a sizable basin for three to four minutes, until they are light and fluffy. Beat in sour cream and vanilla after adding each egg one at a time, just until incorporated.

2. The following are the results of the survey. Beat in the dry ingredients after gradually incorporating the wet ones.

3. To make streusel, mix brown sugar, flour, cinnamon, nutmeg, and salt in a medium basin. Add butter and, if using, pecans.

4. Spread an even layer of batter over the prepared baking pan after adding half the batter. Place half of the streusel on top, then pour remaining batter on top and spread to pan's edges. Add the remaining streusel on top, then bake for 50 to 55 minutes, or until a toothpick inserted in the center comes out clean.

34. BEST-EVER CREAMY SCRAMBLED EGGS

PREP TIME: 5 mins

TOTAL TIME: 8 mins

Ingredients

- 2 large eggs
- 2 tsp. Greek yogurt (2% or whole)
- 1/2 tbsp. butter

- 2 tsp. freshly chop up chives
- Kosher salt
- Freshly ground black pepper

Directions

1. Using a fork, mix the eggs and yogurt in a medium bowl.
2. Melt butter in a medium nonstick pan over low heat. Add eggs once the butter has melted fully. When the eggs begin to set, gently jiggle the cooked egg in the pan using a rubber spatula. Fold in chives when the eggs are almost done cooking to your preference before plating. Add salt and pepper as need.

35. CRESCENT BREAKFAST SQUARES

PREP TIME:10 mins

TOTAL TIME:1 hr

Ingredients

- 12 large eggs
- 1/4 c. milk
- 3 tbsp. butter, separated
- Kosher salt
- Freshly ground black pepper
- 2 cans crescent dough
- 1/2 lb. deli ham, split
- 1/4 c. lightly chop up chives
- 12 slices cheddar
- 1 tsp. poppy seeds
- 1 tsp. sesame seeds
- 1 tsp. chop up onion

- 1 tsp. dried garlic
- Flaky sea salt

Directions

1. Grease a baking sheet with cooking spray and preheat the oven to 375 degrees. Eggs and milk should be whisked together in a big bowl.

2. 1 tbsp of butter should be melted over medium heat in a sizable nonstick pan. Add egg mixture after lowering heat to low once butter has foamed. Sauté, stirring constantly with a spatula, until eggs are just set. Add salt and pepper, then turn off the heat.

3. On a prepared baking sheet, unroll one can of crescents and pinch the seams together to form a continuous layer of pastry with no gaps. Ham should be layered on top, followed by scrambled eggs, cheese, and chives. Place the second crescent dough roll, unrolled, on top of the cheese. To seal the crescents, pinch them together.

4. Melt any leftover butter in the microwave. Poppy seeds, sesame seeds, chop up onion, and dried garlic are sprinkled on top of the crescent dough after it has been brushed with melted butter. Add sea salt, the flaky kind.

5. Bake for 25 to 30 minutes, or until the crescent dough is golden and cooked through. (Use foil to protect the crescent dough if it is browning too soon.)

6. It is a good idea to have a backup plan in case something goes wrong.

36. EASTER BREAD

PREP TIME:15 mins

TOTAL TIME:3 hrs 30 mins

Ingredients

FOR THE BREAD

- 1 c. lukewarm milk
- 1/2 c. + 1 tsp. granulated sugar, separated
- 2 1/2 tsp. or 1 (0.25-oz.) package active dry yeast
- 4 1/2 c. all-purpose flour, + more for surface
- 2 tsp. kosher salt
- 2 large eggs
- 1/2 c. (1 stick) butter, softened and slice into cubes

- Egg wash, for brushing
- Sprinkles, for topping

FOR THE EGGS

- 4 large eggs
- 1 c. boiling water, separated
- 2 tsp. distilled white vinegar, separated
- Food coloring

Directions

1. Spray some frying oil in a big bowl. Add milk, 1 tsp sugar, and yeast to a small bowl or liquid measuring cup of. Let to settle for 8 minutes or until foamy.

2. Mix the flour, salt, and remaining 1/2 cup of sugar in the bowl of a stand mixer equipped with the dough hook. Add eggs and the milk and yeast mixture. For about 5 minutes, mix until a fairly soft dough develops. Butter should be added at a rate of one tbsp at a time, mixing thoroughly after each addition, until the dough comes away from the sides of the bowl, which should take about 15 minutes.

3. Put the dough to a greased bowl, cover it, and let it in a warm place to rise for 1 to 1 1/2 hours, or until doubled in size.

4. Make hard-boiled eggs in the interim: Put the eggs in a medium pot and add water to cover them. Bring to a boil over medium heat. Shift the heat off and cover. 11 minutes later, remove from pan and submerge in icy water.

5. Give each bowl a cup of the boiling water. Each bowl should contain 1 tsp vinegar and the specified food coloring. If desired color, add one egg at a time and let sit for 5 to 10 minutes. To remove from the bowl and let dry, use a slotted spoon. Place a wire rack over a baking sheet.

6. Put parchment paper on a sizable baking sheet and preheat the oven to 375 degrees. Divide dough into three equal pieces and place on a lightly dusted surface. Each component should be rolled into a 16" rope. On the prepared baking sheet, arrange the ropes lengthwise side by side. After tightly braiding the ropes together, pinch the upper ends together. Pinch the ends together after circling the ends.

7. Incorporate colored eggs into the braid, cover the dough, and allow it to double in size for about 30 minutes.

8. Brush with egg wash and top with sprinkles. Bake for 30 minutes, or until brown.

37. INSTANT POT HASH

PREP TIME:15 mins

TOTAL TIME: 50 mins

Ingredients

- 1 tbsp. extra-virgin olive oil
- 1 tbsp. butter
- 1/2 lb. thick-slice Canadian bacon
- 1/2 medium yellow onion, chop up
- 1 red bell pepper, chop up
- 1 green bell pepper, chop up
- 2 cloves garlic, chop up
- 1 tsp. dried oregano
- 1/2 tsp. cumin seeds (non-compulsory)
- 1/4 tsp. cayenne
- Kosher salt
- Freshly ground black pepper
- 1 lb. yellow potatoes, quartered
- 1/2 c. low-sodium vegetable broth
- 1 tbsp. freshly chop up parsley, for garnish
- Eggs, for serving

Directions

1. Sauté on medium in the Instant Pot. Add butter and oil to the pot. After butter is melted, fry bacon until crisp. Add the peppers and onions, and sauté until the vegetables are soft.

2. Add cayenne, cumin seeds, oregano, garlic, and oregano, if using. Add salt and pepper, and simmer for 1 minute, or until the spices and garlic are aromatic.

3. Add potatoes and broth to pot and stir to mix. Set the pressure in the Instant Pot. Set the timer for 12 minutes and cook on high. Use the rapid release technique to release pressure when the timer goes off.

4. Lift the lid, then switch the Instant Pot back to Sauté. Boil for about 2 minutes, stirring regularly, or until all of the broth has evaporated.

5. Serve with fried eggs and parsley as a garnish.

38. MONTE CRISTO SANDWICH

PREP TIME: 15 mins

TOTAL TIME: 30 mins

Ingredients

- 4 large eggs
- 1/2 c. whole milk
- 1 tsp. kosher salt
- 8 tsp. Dijon mustard
- 8 slices white sandwich bread
- 8 oz. split Swiss cheese
- 6 oz. deli ham
- 6 oz. deli turkey
- 4 tbsp. unsalted butter, separated
- Confectioners' sugar and raspberry preserves, for serving

Directions

1. Preheat oven to 200°. A baking sheet with a wire rack inside should be placed in the oven to heat up. In a large bowl, whisk eggs, milk, and salt until completely incorporated.

2. Put a thin amount of mustard on one side of each slice of bread. Cover half of bread pieces with cheese, ham, turkey, and another slice of cheese. Close sandwiches with leftover bread.

3. In a large nonstick skillet over medium-low heat, cook 2 tbsp butter until melted. Working 2 at a time, dip sandwiches into batter to coat, then place in skillet and cook, rotating once, until golden and cheese is melted, 4 to 6 minutes per side. Put to rack in oven to keep warm. Repeat with remaining 2 tbsp butter and sandwiches.

4. Distribute sandwiches among plates. Sprinkle with confectioners' sugar and serve with preserves alongside.

39. BREAKFAST STRATA

PREP TIME: 20 mins

TOTAL TIME: 1 hr 20 mins

Ingredients

- 1 tbsp. butter
- 1 lb. ground Italian sausage
- 10 large eggs
- 2 c. whole milk
- Kosher salt
- Freshly ground black pepper
- 4 c. cubed bread
- 1 1/2 c. shredded Fontina, separated
- 1 c. refrigeratedd spinach, defrosted, drained, and chop up
- 1 c. split baby Bella mushrooms
- 1 c. halved grape tomatoes
- 1/4 c. torn basil, for garnish

Directions

1. Butter should be used to oil a 9" x 13" baking dish. Sausage should be cooked for about 7 minutes over medium-high heat, breaking up any large chunks with a spoon while it cooks. Turn off the heat and allow to cool.

2. Add salt and pepper to the mixture of milk and eggs in the big bowl. Add the bread, 1 cup of cheese, spinach, mushrooms, tomatoes, and cooked sausage using gentle motions.

3. Fill baking dish with mixture. Add the final 1/2 cup of cheese on top, then bake for 50 to 55 minutes, or until the cheese is browned and no liquid is visible. Basil should be garnished before serving.

40. SOUR CREAM COFFEE CAKE

PREP TIME: 15 mins

TOTAL TIME: 1 hr 45 mins

Ingredients

FOR THE CAKE

- 3 c. all-purpose flour
- 2 tsp. baking powder
- 1 tsp. kosher salt
- 1/2 tsp. baking soda
- 3/4 c. (1 1/2 sticks) butter, softened
- 1 c. packed light brown sugar
- 1/2 c. granulated sugar
- 3 large eggs
- 2 tsp. pure vanilla extract
- 1 1/2 c. sour cream
- 3/4 c. buttermilk

FOR THE STREUSEL

- 3/4 c. packed light brown sugar
- 3/4 c. all-purpose flour
- 1 tbsp. ground cinnamon
- Pinch kosher salt
- 1/2 c. (1 stick) cold butter, slice into cubes

Directions

1. To prepare the batter, preheat the oven to 350 degrees and spray cooking spray in a bundt pan. Mix the flour, baking soda, salt, and baking powder in a big bowl.

2. In another large bowl using a hand mixer, or in the bowl of a stand mixer with the paddle attachment, beat butter and sugars until light and fluffy, 3 to 4 minutes. One at a time, beat well after each egg addition before adding vanilla. About half of the dry ingredients should be added to the bowl; stir until just a few dry streaks are visible. Stir in buttermilk and sour cream after adding them. Mix just until mixed before adding the last of the dry ingredients.

3. To make streusel, mix sugar, flour, cinnamon, and a dash of salt in a medium basin. When the mixture is pea-sized and beginning to resemble sand, add butter and slice into it with your fingertips.

4. an if you if you if you the if you if you if you if you if you if you a the a that a. Spread the remaining cake batter in a uniform layer on top. The remaining streusel should be placed on top, followed by an even layer of the remaining cake batter.

5. Bake for 50 to 60 minutes, or until brown and a toothpick inserted in the center comes out clean. Let to cool for ten minutes, then flip over onto a cooling rack to finish cooling.

41. CLASSIC CINNAMON ROLLS

PREP TIME:30 mins

TOTAL TIME:3 hrs 25 mins

Ingredients

FOR THE DOUGH

- 1 c. warm milk
- 2 1/4 tsp. or 1 (0.25-oz.) packet instant yeast
- 2 large eggs, at room temperature
- 5 tbsp. butter, softened
- 4 1/2 c. all-purpose flour
- 2 tsp. kosher salt
- 1/2 c. granulated sugar
- 1/4 tsp. baking soda

FOR THE FILLING

- 1/2 c. (1 stick) butter, softened
- 3/4 c. packed brown sugar
- 2 tbsp. ground cinnamon
- 1/2 tsp. ground nutmeg
- 1/2 tsp. kosher salt

FOR THE FROSTING

- 6 oz. cream cheese, softened
- 1/2 c. (1 stick) butter, softened
- 1 c. powdered sugar
- Pinch kosher salt

- 1 tsp. pure vanilla extract
- 1/4 c. milk or heavy cream

Directions

1. Cooking spray should be used to lightly coat a big bowl and a 9" x 13" pan. Mix milk and yeast using a dough hook in a separate big basin or the bowl of a stand mixer until the yeast is mostly dissolved. On low speed, add the remaining dough ingredients. For 15 to 18 minutes, mix at medium-high speed until a smooth, soft dough forms and begins to pull away from the bowl's sides. Rotate the dough in the greased bowl to thoroughly grease the outside. Let to rise for one and a half to two hours, covered with a kitchen towel.

2. Make the filling in the interim: Butter, sugar, cinnamon, nutmeg, and salt should be mixd in a large basin with a hand mixer and creamed for 3 to 4 minutes, or until light and fluffy.

3. 400° oven preheat. On a surface that has been lightly dusted with flour, transfer the dough. Roll out into a roughly 18" × 18" square. Distribute the filling to the border of the dough, roll it into a log, and slice it into 12 pieces that are each approximately 1 1/2" wide.

4. Rolls should be placed slice side up in the baking pan. Let to rise once more for 30 to 40 minutes, then cover.

5. Bake for 20 to 22 minutes, or until brown.

6. of. the the the the the of of of the Butter and cream cheese should be mixd in a big bowl and beat until frothy. Beat in the vanilla, salt, and powdered sugar until smooth. To loosen the frosting, gradually add milk (or heavy cream).

7. After the cinnamon rolls are done baking, immediately frost them. Serve hot.

42. LEMON BLUEBERRY BABKA

PREP TIME:20 mins

TOTAL TIME:4 hrs

Ingredients

FOR THE BREAD

- 1/2 c. lukewarm whole milk

- 1/4 c. granulated sugar, + 1 tsp, separated
- 1 (0.25-oz.) package active dry yeast
- 2 3/4 c. all-purpose flour, + more for surface
- 1 tsp. kosher salt
- 2 large eggs
- 1 tsp. pure vanilla extract
- Zest of 1 large lemon
- 4 tbsp. butter, softened, + more for pan

FOR THE BLUEBERRY FILLING

- 2 c. fresh or refrigeratedd blueberries
- 1/4 c. granulated sugar
- Juice of 1/2 lemon
- FOR THE LEMON GLAZE
- 1/2 c. powdered sugar
- Juice and zest of 1/2 lemon

Directions

1. To make dough, mix milk and 1 tsp sugar in a big glass measuring cup of. Add the yeast and wait 5 minutes for it to froth.

2. Mix the flour, salt, and remaining 1/4 cup of sugar in the bowl of a stand mixer equipped with the dough hook. Add the eggs, vanilla, lemon zest, and yeast mixture. Stir on medium speed until a smooth dough develops and starts to climb up the dough hook and slaps sides of bowl, at least 5 minutes. Butter should be added in increments of roughly 1 tbsp, waiting until each addition has been fully absorbed.

3. Turn dough into a medium bowl that has been greased with butter. Depending on how warm your kitchen is, let the dough rise for 1 to 2 hours while covered with a clean kitchen towel.

4. Make the blueberry filling in the interim: Blueberries, sugar, and lemon juice are mixd in a medium saucepan over medium heat. Simmer for 10 to 12 minutes, stirring frequently, until the blueberries are mostly broken down and the mixture begins to thicken. Let to totally cool.

Made in United States
Troutdale, OR
04/14/2025